PAINT BY STICKER
STICKER KIDS
UNDER THE SEA

workman
• NEW YORK •

The following images were used to create the low-poly interpretations in this book:

Page 5: Dolphin
© allorate/fotolia

Page: 7: Star Fish
© Martin Wilkinson/fotolia

Page 9: Clownfish
© julialine802/fotolia

Page 11: Jellyfish
© Pavlo Vakhrushev/fotolia

Page 13: Narwhal
© Field Museum Library/Getty Images

Page 15: Sea Turtle
© isabelle_bonaire/fotolia

Page 17 School of Fish
© leonardogonzalez/fotolia

Page 19: Deep Sea Diver
© Hulton Archive/Getty Images

Page 21 and Cover: Octopus
© dxc/Graphic River

Page 23: Sunken Boat
© Danita Delimont/Getty Images

ISBN 978-1-5235-0038-3

Concept: Daniel Nayeri, Colleen AF Venable, Phil Conigliaro, Tae Won Yu, Justin Krasner
Art by Phil Conigliaro
Layout & design by Tae Won Yu and Carolyn Bahar
Art direction by Colleen AF Venable
Cover design by Colleen AF Venable, Tae Won Yu, and Carolyn Bahar
Editing by Daniel Nayeri
Production editing by Amanda Hong
Production manager Julie Primavera

Workman books are available at special discounts when purchased in bulk for premiums and sales promotions as well as for fundraising or educational use. Special editions or book excerpts can also be created to specification. For details, contact the Special Sales Director at the address below, or send an email to specialmarkets@workman.com.

Workman Publishing Co., Inc.
225 Varick Street
New York, NY 10014-4381

workman.com

WORKMAN and PAINT BY STICKER are registered trademarks of Workman Publishing Co., Inc.

Printed in China
First printing April 2017
10 9 8 7

INTRODUCTION

IT'S FAIRLY SIMPLE, ACTUALLY. You could try it even now, in your mind. Imagine a sticker. You know stickers, right? The sticky bits of paper? Yes? Good.

Okay, you're peeling a sticker from the sticker sheet. It has a number by it: **31**. That's easy to remember. **31**. You take the sticker to the art page. On the page is the outline of a starfish, or a sea turtle, or an octopus. Inside the outline is a web of delicate shapes—as if a spider drew you a picture.

All you have to do is find **31**. It's over . . . *there*. You place the sticker onto the space. It's as if you filled the space with a perfectly even coat of paint. You brought color to the world. It might be the orange fin of a clown fish or the pink coral beside a sunken ship.

It's a magical feeling. You could do it again. You could paint the whole image. It'd be yours. Don't worry if the lines are a bit off. They look like the irregular stones in a mosaic.

GO AHEAD. YOU'RE A NATURAL.

TIPS TO GET YOU STARTED:

1. The sticker sheets are assigned to each art page by the thumbnail images in the top corners of the sticker sheets.

2. Use the perforations to tear out either the art page or the sticker sheets so you don't have to flip back and forth in the book.

3. Go in any order you like. You're the boss.

4. Place one corner of the sticker down and adjust from there. Be careful; these stickers are not removable.

5. For precision placement, use a toothpick or tweezers.

6. After you complete an image, place a sheet of paper over it and press down with a flat surface, like a ruler or bone folder.

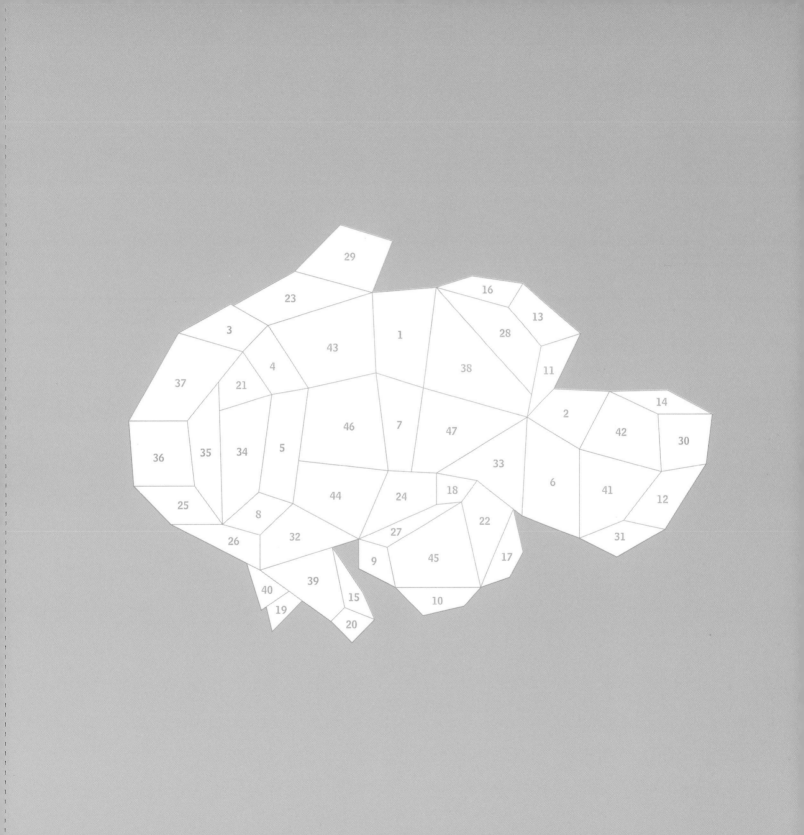

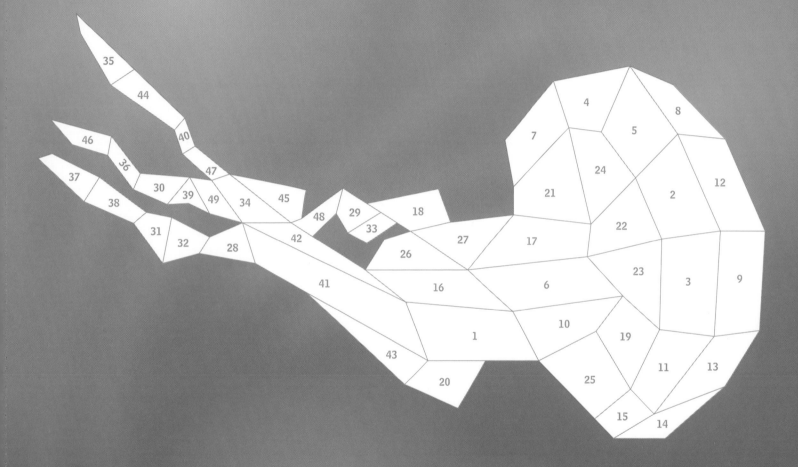

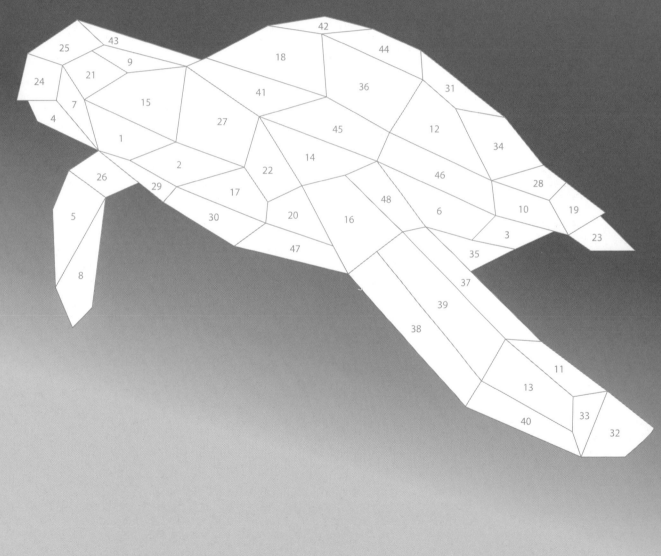

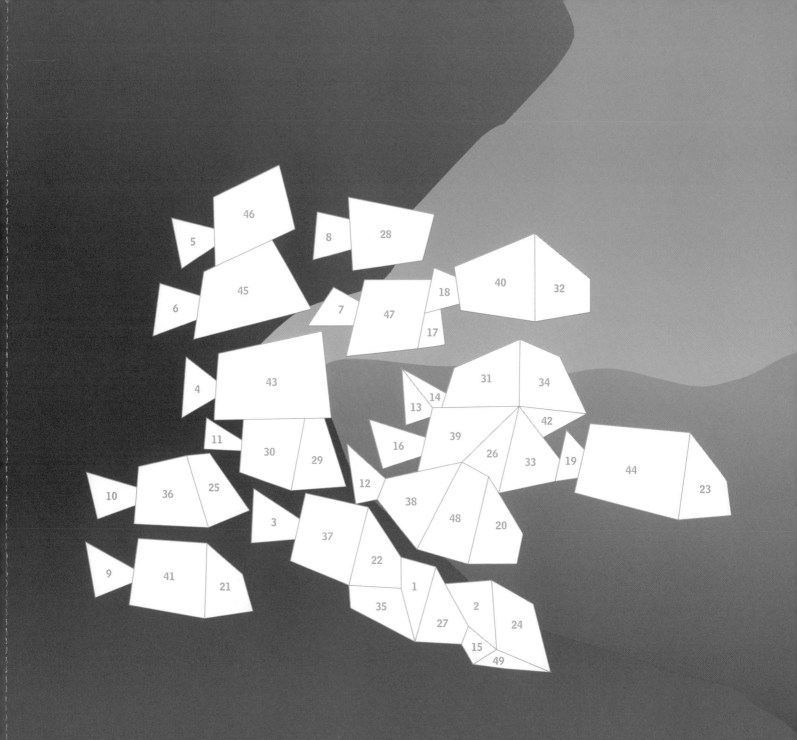

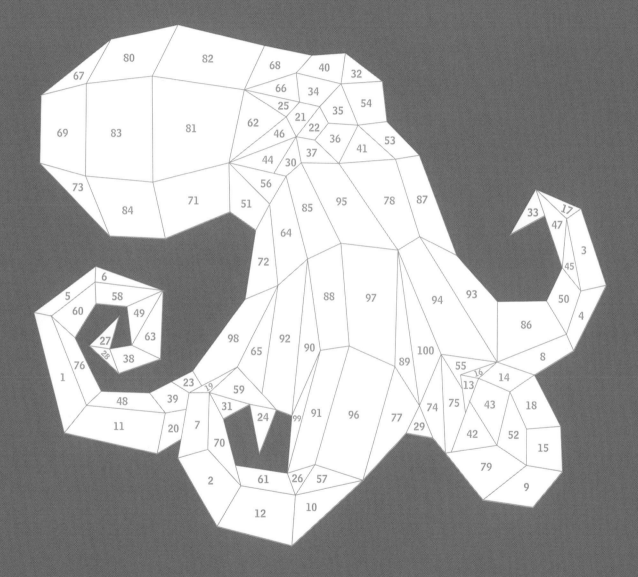

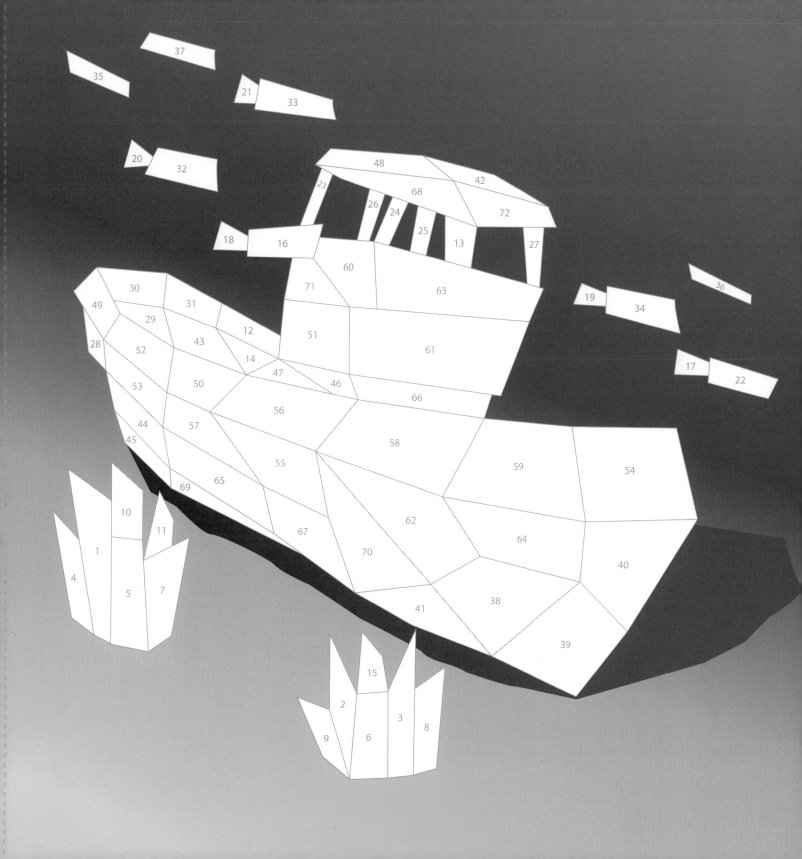

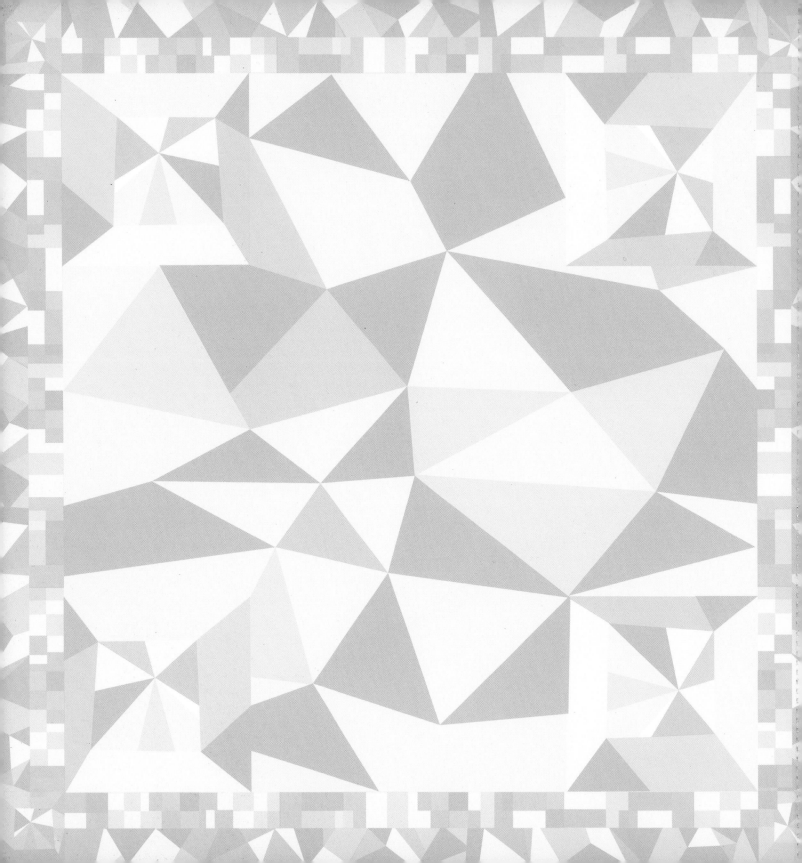

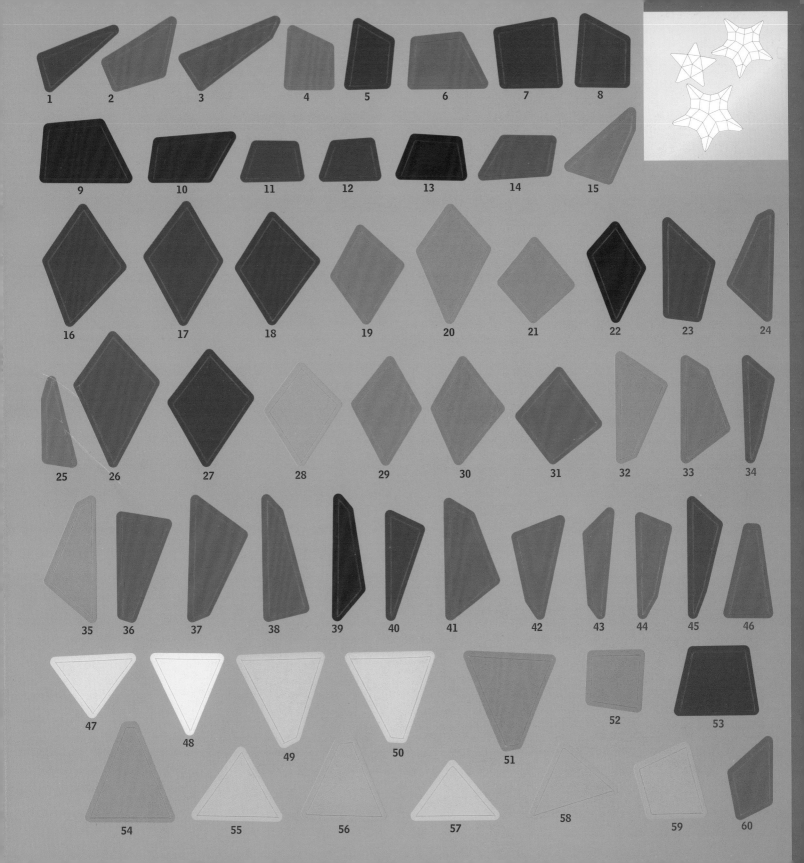

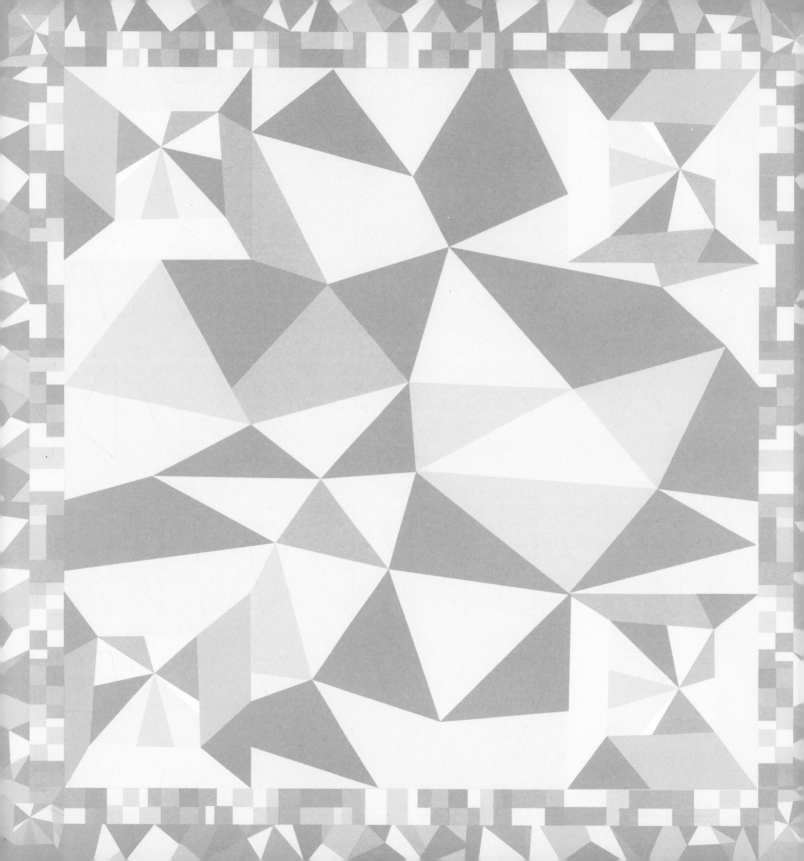

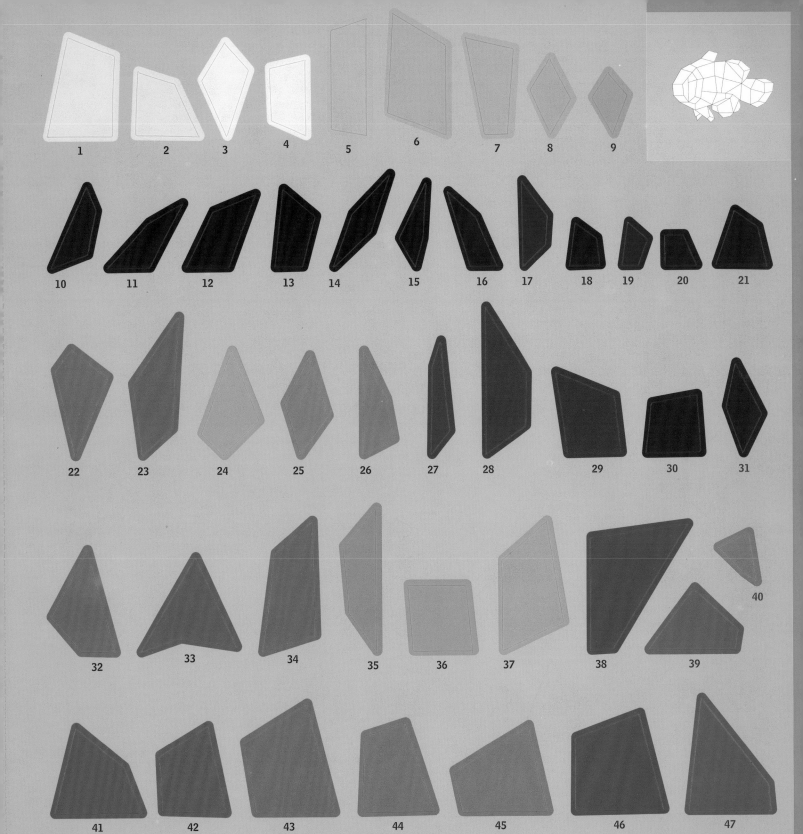

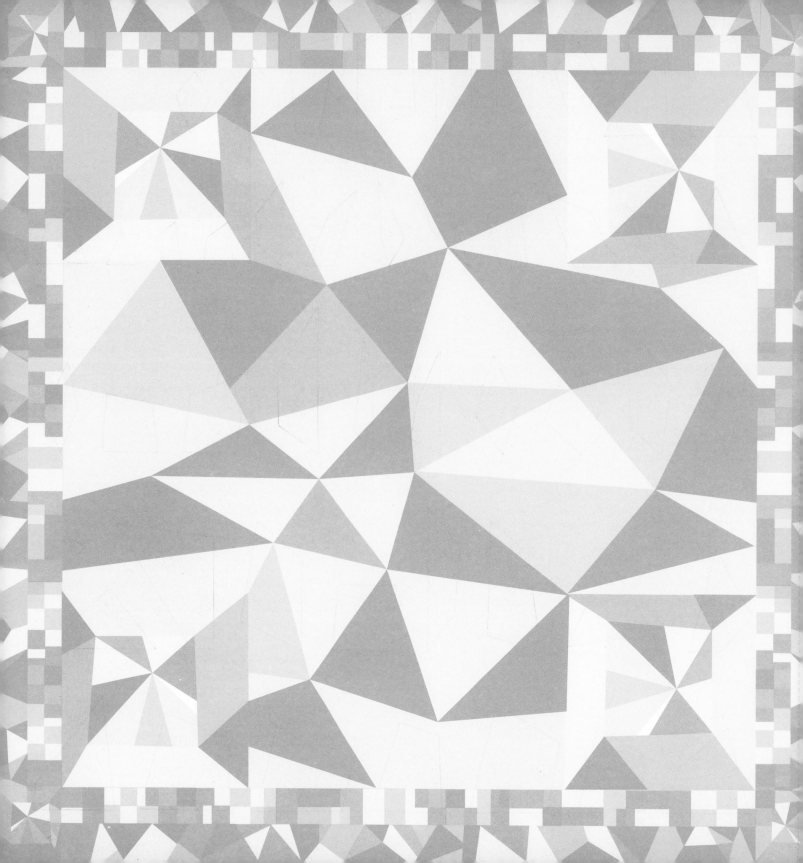

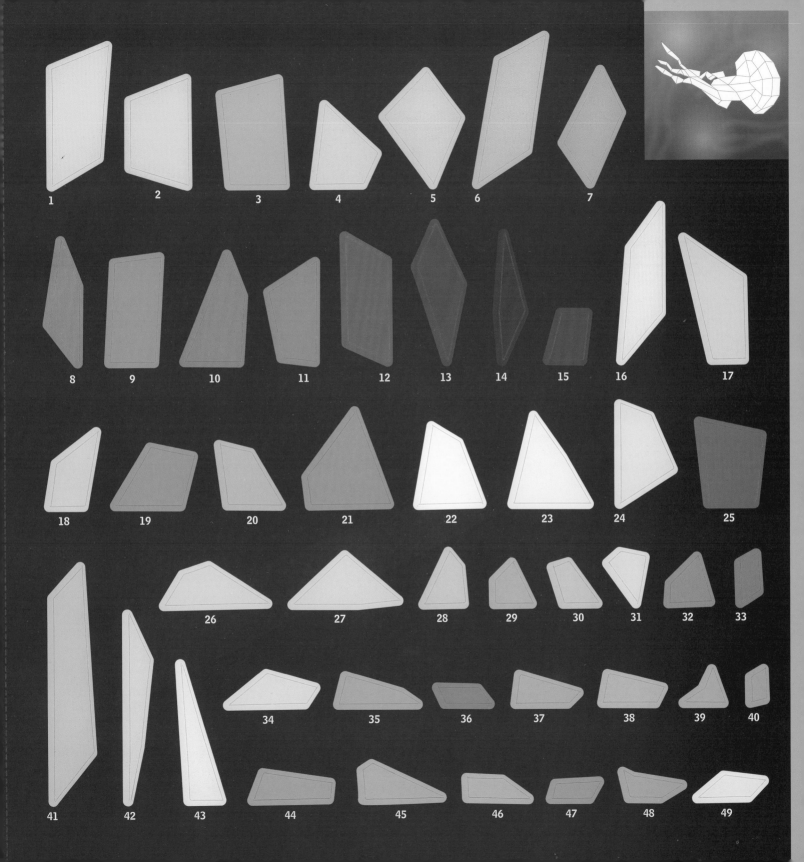

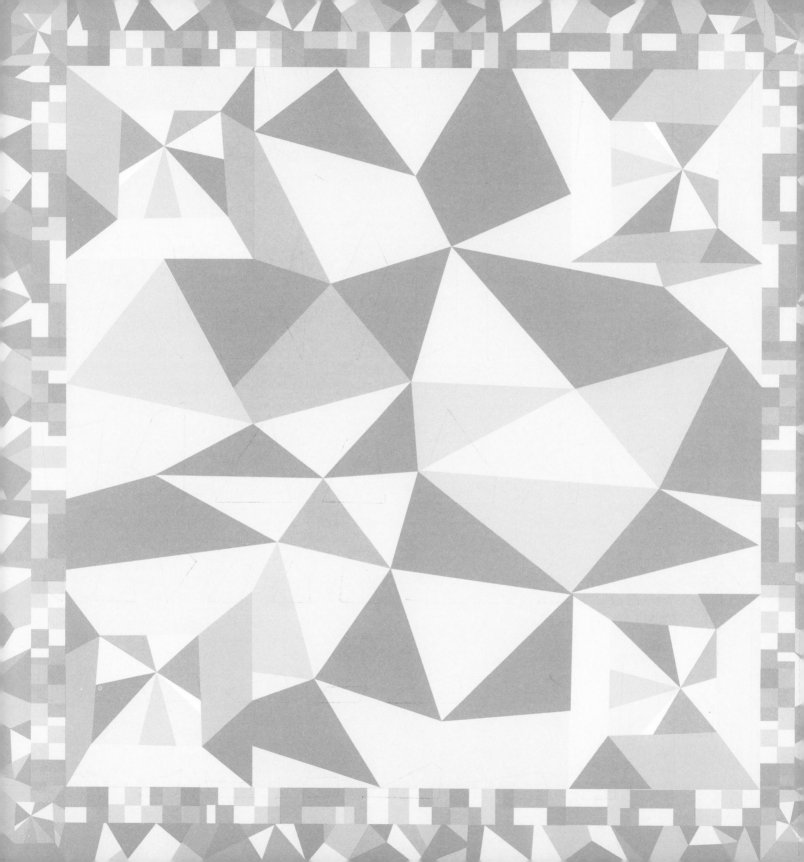

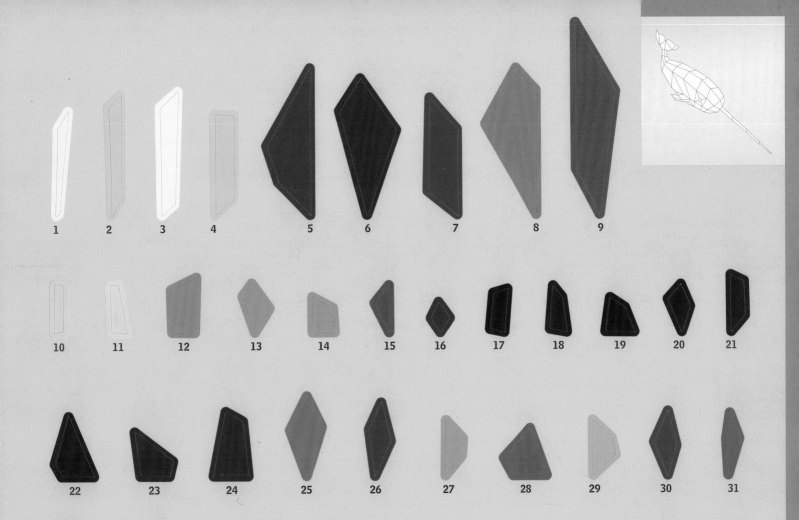

1   2   3   4   5   6   7   8   9

10   11   12   13   14   15   16   17   18   19   20   21

22   23   24   25   26   27   28   29   30   31

32   33   34   35   36   37   38   39   40

41   42   43   44   45   46   47   48

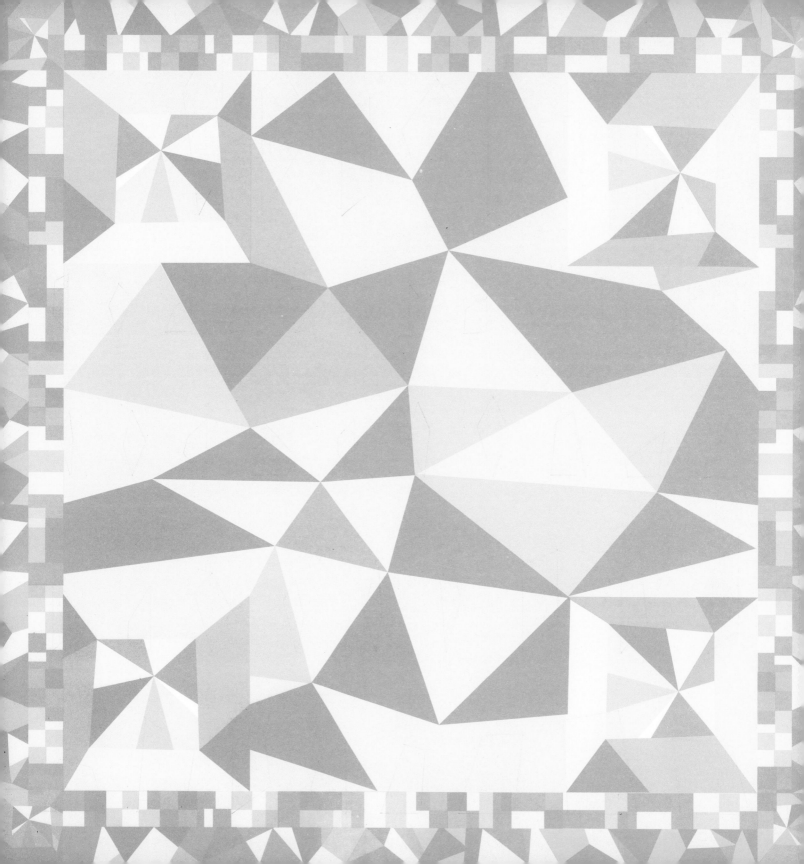

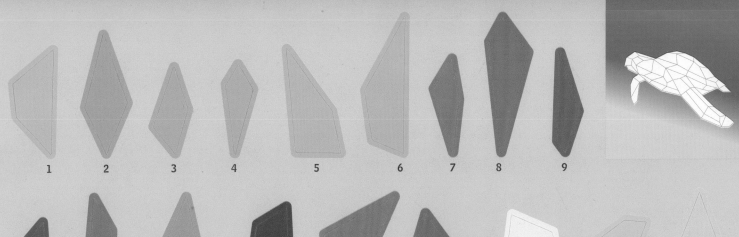

1   2   3   4   5   6   7   8   9

10   11   12   13   14   15   16   17   18

19   20   21   22   23   24   25   26

27   28   29   30   31   32   33   34   35   36

37   38   39   40   41   42   43   44   45   46   47   48

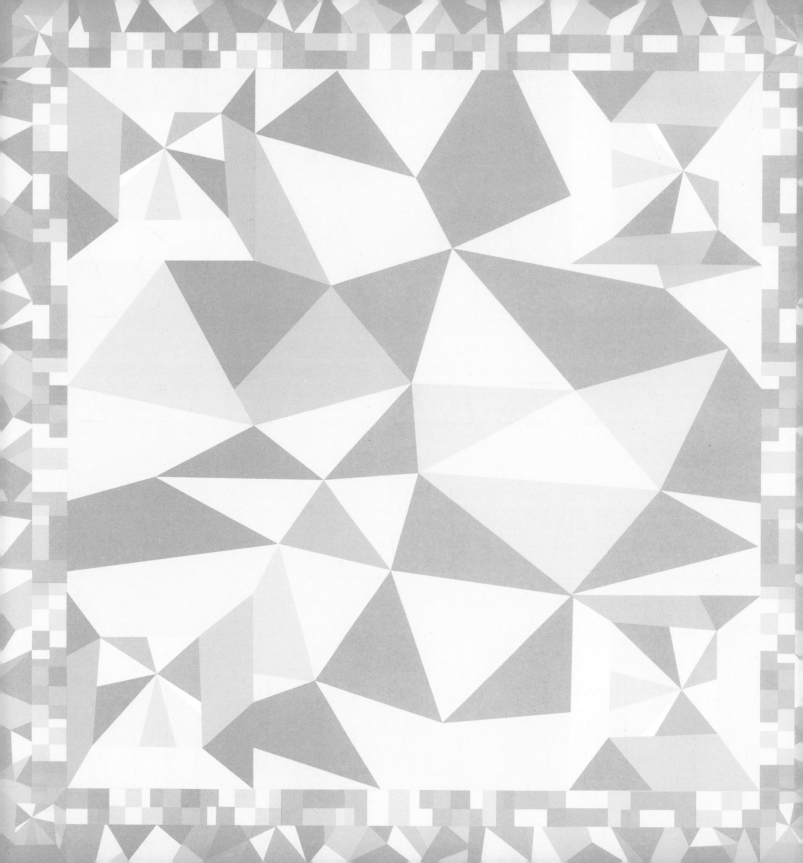

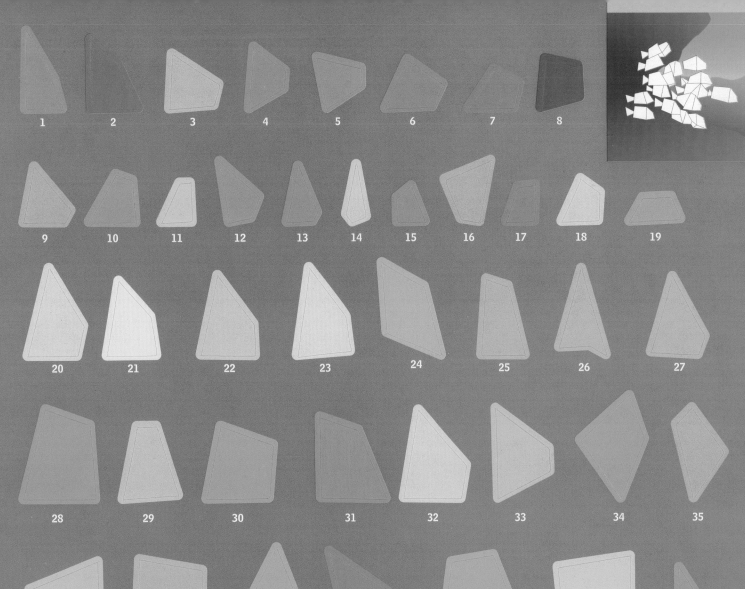

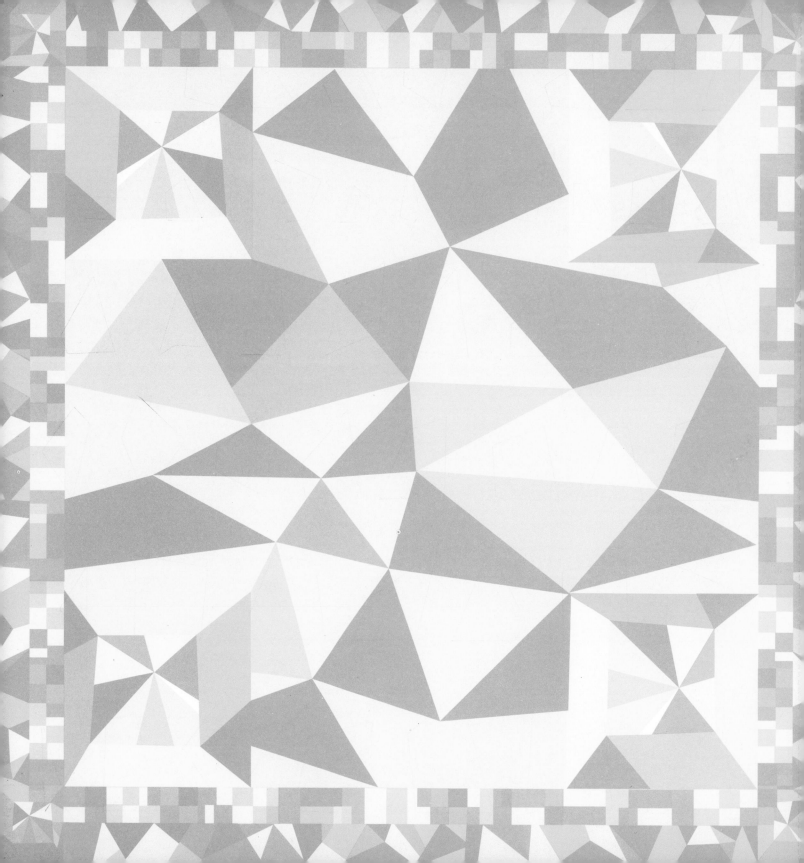

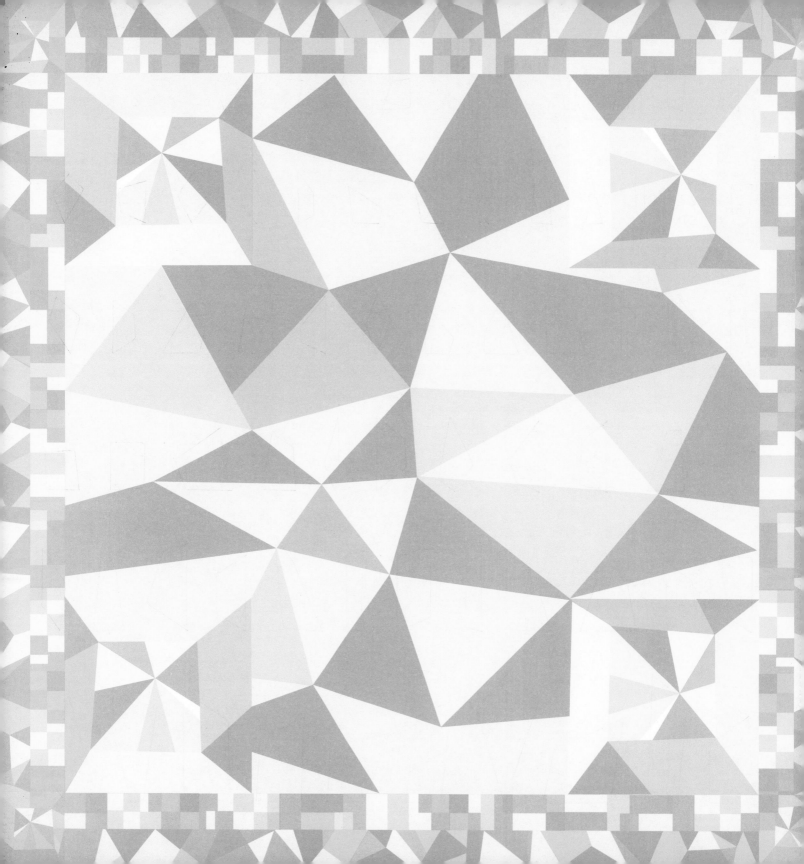

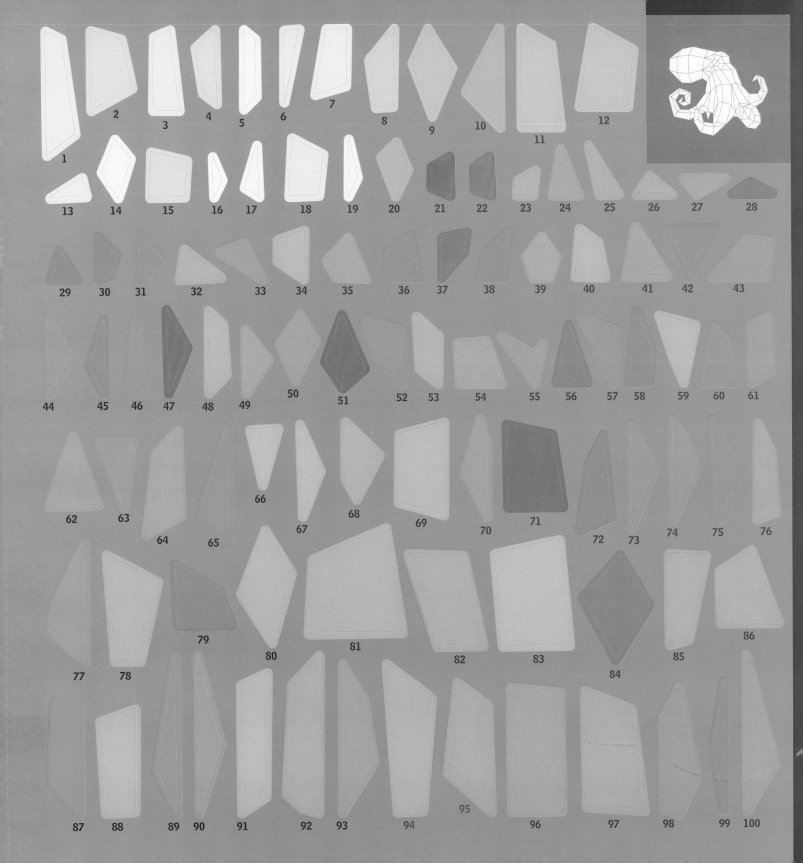

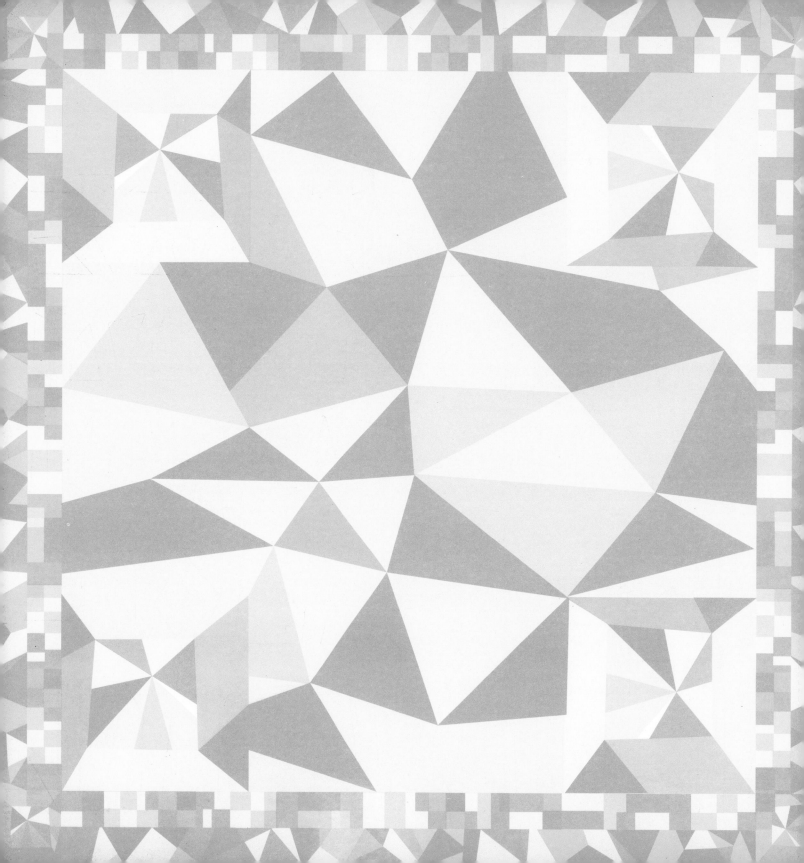

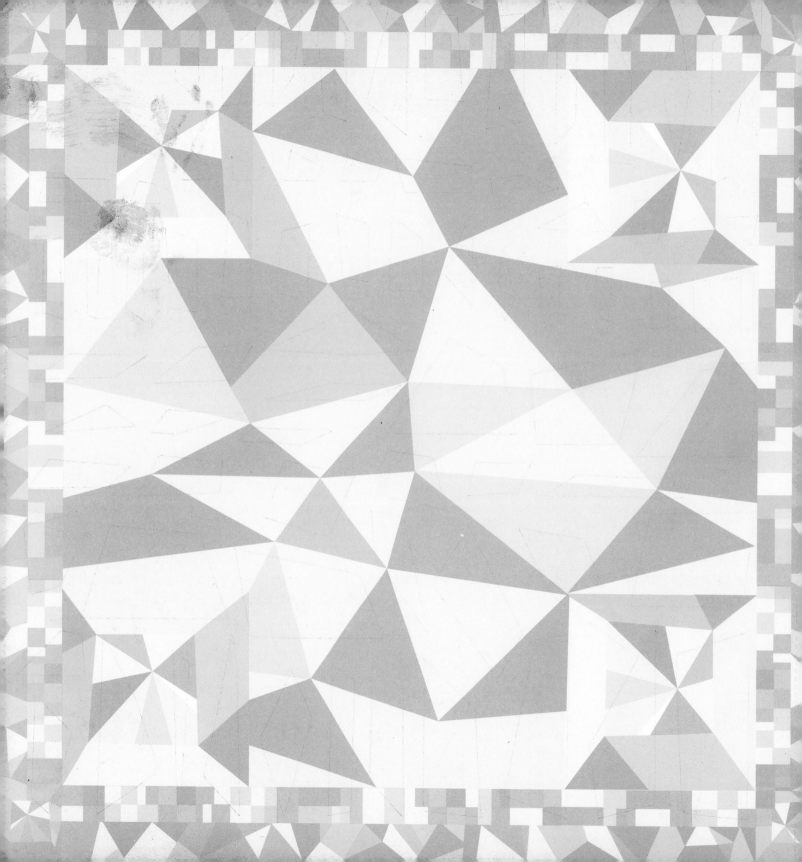